ASTRS

53 SP 37

December 2021
Brooklyn, NY

ASTRS
© Karinne Keithley Syers 2021
53rdstatepress.org

ISBN Number: 9780997866483
Library of Congress Number: 2021931720

Book design: Karinne Keithley Syers
Cover art: Sara Smith

Printed on recycled paper in the United States of America.

ASTRS

written by Karinne Keithley Syers
drawings by Sara Smith

53rd State Press
Brooklyn, NY

Note on the text

This text is a libretto to be spoken, sung and projected.
The division of words between those seen and those
heard, those spoken and those sung, should be deter-
mined within the rehearsal process and can change according to the configuration of collaborating performers
and designers. The elements (projection, speech and song)
will mostly alternate, but may be at times simultaneous,
so that there is an accretion of layers that moves musical-
ly and rhythmically alongside the accretion of narrative
sense.

Included somehow in the visual scheme should be
drawings diagramming Louis Auguste Blanqui's vision
of the endlessly bifurcating cosmos described in his book
L'eternité par les astres and meditated upon by Walter
Benjamin in his *Arcades Project*.

Shifts of space and vocal parts are not indicated in the
text, except for the broad division of the text into four
sections. The orchestration of voices is rather expected
to be part of the process of developing a specific performance. As a starting point, an ensemble of three or four

people can read the text, trading off at each paragraph break and speaking or singing in unison where text is italicized. The text is dense if approached with constant forward momentum. Staging the play will involve the question of tempo, and I hope anyone attempting to stage this play, even just speculatively in their reading mind, will feel free to move at various speeds, to pool here and there for a rest, to gather here and there for an attack.

In addition to musical thinking, it's useful to think of the narrative structure of this thing as a kind of mural, in which everything is always happening at once in the same picture plane. I used to variously subtitle it "a rabbit cosmogony" (though it is a world without beginnings) or "a militant rabbit folk opera" or a "radio play folk opera duck animation with dances," and now, fifteen years after it was first written, it has become a sacred text, "The Book of ASTRS," for the lonely rabbit who populates Chrysanthemum Square (another radio play with dances), an astrogardener drifting the lined interior of outerspace boredom. You are invited to invent and embrace your own explanation.

Part 1

Look at the stars. Just look at them.

The rabbit is pleading for his life.

O one. O might have been.

You people. Says the rabbit. You people spend your lives in the company of dead things.

You flash back. All the way back to the origin of species. To the very first pebble of the endless piling up of things. There. It's out of you. It's gone.

Mr. Augustus B. Rabbit is looking at the stars. Gazing upon the endless unfolding of bifurcating universes. "All that one might have been in this world, one is in another."

Cosmicspliternity. In a yellow wood. In a darksome distant galaxy.

Plop, pellet, walk, talk, plop at the same time. Sure, the rabbit can do it all. But at this instant, Mr. A. B. Rabbit isn't walking. Or even hopping. He is stopped dead in his tracks.

Just ahead of him a wildebeest is pointing at a snail who is pointing at a deer who is pointing at a gun which is trained on Augustus B. Rabbit who stares

starestarificating rabbit. Contemplates in a long and timeless present, the infinite bifurcations of possible worlds.

"All that one might have been in this world, one is in another."

And yet—in the unfolding of particulars—condemned to be in this one—only—at every instance of possibility. Only this one.

Rabbit brainwaves across the space field. See Rabbit send psychic signals to his double on another planet where he won't, in a second, be

                    [bang, the rabbit is down]

dead. Now you are in the company of a dead thing.

Of a dead thing.

Welcome to the 53rd State of the Union. Welcome to the zone of the sixth chrysanthemum. Welcome to the frozen duck pond. It is the ice age.

Here in the icy wastes of the 53rd State, the hunter is pointing at the deer.

> *yr necksd*

says the hunter

> *no yrrr necksd*

snarls the dear

This is the beginning of the middle of the beginning, the end of the middle of the start of things, when—

WAIT FOR IT

boredom boredom boredom boredom
lined interior of boredom

Now.

What if the rabbit who stared at the stars on a freezing day, with turns philosophical, near the iceaged duckpond of the 53rd State of the Union, upon whom icy death fixed unshakeable stare whilst distant planets bifurcate, with all possibilities gaining a world, YET Augustus B. Rabbit is doomed to live in this one, WHAT IF the rabbit

was the revolutionary leader of a great and fearsome militia?

Well he was.

Pan in on furious tattooed rabbit brigade.

A band of terrorrabbits.

Who's necksd? Yrrr necksd.

Menacingly.

Swarm of wild rabbits descends upon the city at twilight. It's one o'clock in the morning. It's the frozen world.

It was a time of great destruggtion.

Nothing is left standing. Blood runs in the streets. A storm blows out of paradise and sweeps the vagabondits into the icy river.

brk ckckckckckckck and then,

You think back, to the end of the middle of the beginning, to the origin of species. You flash, all in an instant. To the earliest future of categories, the first and smallest differentiation. You think back to the windmill fantasy. To the urisistible urphenomenon.

The foxhounds will be eaten by the fox.

We are building cities we cannot live in. We have lost our alphabet and must learn to draw again. We have run over our own toes with tanks, and yet tippy tippy tip toe dancing refuses to die. Demands can't be met. They must be broken.

The white light got frozen. The lightyear calculator has a glitch.

These are times when hope is less robust, less like a balloon and more like a cigarette. The rabbit militia has eaten everything in this world.

"We know of the possibility of other worlds. But we are indissolubly bound to this one."

No one can think on their toes anymore. The end times can't seem to wrap it up and the middle times hang around eternally. Enter Sibyl Kempson from another dimension.

Sibyl Kempson rides across the land on her horse. She draws back a magnificent arrow and shoots a magnificent moon. On the way, the arrow skewers the ice age and so spring springs again. The arrow carries the ice age across the cosmonautical wasteland and lands fortyeightthousand lightyears away. The lightyear calculators curse Sibyl Kempson.

"Damn you, Kempson."

And in the duckpond of the 53rd State of the Union, masses of goslings quivering in the green rushes above a still and polleny pond whisper, Sibyl, Sibyl. In fifty-three polyrhythms. Sibyl, Sibyl.

Her horse has led her here to the 53rd State of the Union. It is not far from Pennsylvania.

Meanwhile.
In the capital city, CAPITALISMUSVILLE,
people in green buildings stare out of pink windows.
Then they pull the shades. Dark things are happening in
the duckponds on the edge of town.

(and a wailing chorus of cats went:

mrrroaughhhh
mrrrrrrauggggghhhhhaw
hawweighhaw
hoorrrrmmmmrrrraugh)

In this sorry place, goslings succumb to typhoid fever.
Gosling mothers sneer across the cosmoplane at the
universes where typhoid fever is a disease for trashcans,
not goslings. An aluminum affliction.

This knowledge is torture.

Says Gosling Mom, mother of Gosling Mary. Typhoidal
Mary Gosling swears by the stars above, but the stars
sing, *ha. ha. ha la la.*

Unfortunately, sound being even slower than light, we
will have to wait quite a while before Mary the Typhoidal
Goz registers a response.

WAIT FOR IT

boredom boredom boredom boredom
lined interior of boredom

wait for it

Ten million, three hundred twenty nine thousand, four hundred eighty eight years later:

Sibyl is gone. The gosling has gone under. The music of the stars falls on the ears of dead things.

[COSMOPLANE WALL]

I am a set of words. I am about to undergo a
process of division. I will be taken apart
according to possible recombinations. I am
armed for change. I would like to display
the ways I can be categorized. You will see
that I have within myself rulers, legends,
and conventions. I would like to offer
instructions for a dance. I thank you ahead
of time.

I am a set of words about to. I am undergo.
taken apart I will be a process. of division
categorized, according I am to possible to
display recombinations, the ways I can be.
You will see ahead of time. I would like
legends and conventions armed for change.
I would like to offer instructions for that
I have within myself rulers a dance. I
thank you.

arm categorized words according to nations
comb the ways I display. possible like ed

for change. of division apart. to be to I for am taken about time undergo legends and off conventions. of I would You that will see ahead. I myself rulers of a dance thank you. will I a process set. I am i re I am a can be would like to instruct, er, I have ions within I.

nations rulers thank you. possible like time off words for change set categorized according to process. to be to I for am about undergo legends and of division taken aparted vent con willions. would see my head of self. will I a. i re a I am that a a can to be would like instruct, er, I have ions within I. arm dance of I I I am You. comb the ways I display.

[END COSMOPLANE]

I I miss the duck
like like cowboy wallwallpaper
like the snail dared point at at the deer

Augustus B. Rabbit, revileutionary and militant B.
Rabbit, is one of many many dead things
sunk in the soggy bogs of the 53rd State.

What lies in the bottom in perfect preservation?
Gentle smiles on the faces of dead things.

The ghosts of the smiling dead inhabit porcelain figurines
and wooden-headed dolls. They whisper to Laura Jones
in the dark recesses of the library.

Recurrence.
This is how it is. The living are lost under the thought of
the dead, it never ends. Round the bend, the rabbit militia
descends again.

They prefer not to look. Every single inhabitant of the 53rd State is intensely paranoid. Typhoidal Gosling Mary's haunted grave is sacked. *"Where's the fugging goldenegg?"*

All the lights in the 53rd State of the Union are put out. It is the beginning of the calendar: a day of remembrance.

Meanwhile,
downriver from CAPITALISMUSVILLE,
Prince Maximilian,
"a visitor from another dimmation,"
gets off a small boat and asks to paint your portrait.
You are flattered yet suspicious.
You imagine terrible things.
You make a bad face and Prince Max says

AH!

and takes many notes.
While the lights come back on.
While illumination leaves the sacred crockpots of the clerics.
While rushes cease to quiver.

While everyone becomes reassured about everything:
barbequing and nonsense, tympani of blessed sensation.

All the journalists are asked to leave. A white-nosed lady
moves to the podium and speaks:

"NO LONGER will there be a philosophy of anything!
Relief is the order of the day. Followed closely by eggs
over easy. Cooing will prevail in dovecotes and the foxes
will leave, embarrassed."

Thank the nice lady for abolishing philosophy. Thank her white hair and white nose. But just before everyone can get home to write a nice thank-you letter, the ghoulish horde of rabbits rears its ugly ugliness. Descends upon. Nothing is left alive. Her white nose and white fingers are wormfood. White hair is fishfood, white knees are dogfood, and the rabbits eat white liver, as rabbits are wont to. Never again will anybody mention philosophical abolitionism.

Sadly do the dead resume their stargazing in all corners of the 53rd State of the Union. They are searching for the distant planet, where ghoulish rabbit hordes, just at the moment of their descent, were eradicated by the introduction of red into the color scheme. If only we had waited! Mournful songs go on for a while now:

sing:

lalalaaaaa
la la laaaaaa
hoo hoo hooweie
hoowee hoowaaoowaa
hoo hoo hoooweeeaii
hooooweeee ha laaaeeeo
rimms ba ta laaalaaa
hooweeee ta ta
rrrrrrrrrrrrrrrrrrrroom
vvvvvvvvvvvvvvvvvvvvvvvvvnnnnoonnn
paah

The revolutionary images are removed from the books. The end of the beginning is the end of all things. Red rabbits rebel. Ghouls go green. This equals the middle time. Equals the end of philosophy. This was dispatched by pigeon post. To the cabbage heads of state. And all the alms were taken back, for the meek had inherited a nice lakefront property. They tore each other's eyes out because they could no longer share.

Dare to say, this equals profound tiredness on the part of the gods of Ur. They abandon their posts. They thumb their noses at Gilgamesh and Ganesh. This equals the beginning of the time of division. Dawn is done and only darkness falls on dances.

(and division and multiplication)

and division and inflection

(and inflection and bifurcation)

Cosmicspliternity. In a yellow wood. In a darksome distant galaxy.

This knowledge is torture.

Traces of the moon lady were discovered frequently in the end of time. She had been throwing cheese, according to the ancient art of do-yu-ra. The ancient art of yrr necksd.

A new calendar is begun.

These are the times when hope is less robust. Less like a cigarette and more like the surge of a minor vindication.

And all the lights in the 53rd State are snuffed out, which causes a rash of deaths by electrocution. The current is free and wild and lost to numbers.

In methodological alleatorical

aleatorellogory

It is a possibility, you know. It is possible.

(Sneer, sneert, sneerjt, and every possible translation of sneert.)
This is the end of wallpaper. All mapmaking is declared to be criminal. It is the beginning of an underground

renaissance. The anti-bifurcationists become strong and for a while they are total!

THEY CHANT: *Everything was always happening at once. Everything on top of everything which was on top of everything else.*

In the cosmos, associations ring across distances. In the 53rd State they meet in the corner. Furniture obsession is epidemic. Angles, joints, and folds.

But what of the duck in the other dimmation? How goes his freedom there?

He is haunted each Thursday. In endless recurrence. The shooting, gutting and stuffing plays on repeat in the basement archives of the cosmoverse.
Was something already known?
"Preventatively as such we have locked it up and suffocated it."

To know, but never to travel to.
To imagine, but never to reach.

sing:

la la la
la la laa laa la
la la la
la la laa laa laaaa

But freedom was gone. Things felt calculated: already known, already dead. Big bad boar is not enough. Badness not near enough. Bigness not upon us. The boar runs through the otherworld and commingles with pitbulls.

And nothing was erefull. Everything was awefull. And what came before came again

condemned.

Such sad stories are everywhere wrapped up in brown paper. They are declared unconstitutional by the legislature. They are requested to leave. Tenderfaced lady throws cheese. Across space. She hurtles it through combo amps and into secret places. She hurtles it without a trace.

[COSMOPLANE WALL]

acding cor to process. nations rulers
forthank you. possible change set. ized
categor! like time off words o be o. t
I. for am undergo . abo leg ut ends and
of vision taken par wouldd I vent conated
willions . see my head elf . of s. LL I a.
i re a I am that a a can to be would like
instruct, er, You wit. I have ions within
I. dance of. arm comb the I dis. am I . I
I. playways.

dac or cessing c to pro. hav sible changee
posset. ized categorke! timlie off words.
o be o. t I. for. am rullegabo undergo
endsut of ion vistaken paro wuldd I vent
conated ers willions . seemy head elf of S.
Lial. i re a I amthat a a can to be would
like instruct, er, wit. I ions within I.
of. barm com the I dis/dan wam I . pli I.
ay say: nations thank you for you dance

[END COSMOPLANE]

Things become self-aware and it is bad.

Your many layered company offends me.

The caucus of ghost deer has grown cynical.

Everything becomes objectionable.

This is a tour of the musical planet.
Where plays meticulous antibacterial cheese music.
Green cars of cheerfulness occupy a hotel with no doors.
A survey is taken of man-made lakes, crossbows, and demolition derbies.

In the future, all things will have been distasteful already.
This is a great relief.
The 51st and 52nd were printed wrong.
Then they were voided.
There was a terrorrible war which blew things apart.
Which severed the moment
so to speak.
That was when indivisibility whent out the whindow.
The beginning of the time of differentiation.

That was the era of wallpaper.
This is the era of skypaper.
There are programs that allow this.
There are ways to.
When trains were swappable.
Then you won't have to do it.

Schooling is done forever.
So are
smart people and social commentary.

This is why it can be said to be a benevolent dream time of ringing bells.

O the ghosts are boasting of terrible things laid low in tannin
and how they laid them there themselves.
"with our bare hands, yar"

menacingly

ringtones on static make everything strange again
bottomy dreamtimes

sing:
Yu aare a gull
and also a gull's goat
and in the gull's throat
is a bull
and in the bull's nose
is more time
than anyone ever
did know what to do with
so everyone sneezes
and everything freezes
and gulls without kneeses
are are falling from treeses

It's getting that way.
Yrr necksd.
twitches, whimpers
In green buildings with pink windows.
Under quilted blankets.
twitches, whimpers
After a lot of slow crushing and inwardness.
twitches, whimpers
Young arsonists denounce fire.
There is no hope left—
unless we can get back to the
benevolent dreamtime of ringing bells.

Dream time
is about furniture, you see.
It is about joindering and dovetailing and the corner.

Unspeakable things are broadcast loudly.
Car alarms inspire great ballads of only one chord.
You know it right?
It was terrible.
We left.

Martial law is declared in the 53rd State of the Union.
53rders quiver behind green buildings.
And in the farmhouse near the duckpond:

I am so scared, yknow
am so so scared yknow

Nature dreams the 53rd State. The 53rd State rebels and
shoots nature in the arse.

Then in the necksd.

Deers bell.
They harbour.
Then they hind.
Nothing is outlawed.
I will abandon you.

Everything will give way to the greatness to come.
Prince Maximilian will want to paint your portrait.
You will make a terrible face:
You will be so ugly.

Prince Max's second voyage takes him upriver of
Capitalismusville. Nothing overheard is overhead
anymore. All is down below, down lower than low. Many
of them are shocked. Prince Max couldn't think about
anything else he could be doing. His trusted advisor
however:

I'm OUTTA HERE aiight.

Prince Max: From now on I'm on my own. *Prince Max:*
I'm not qualified. *Prince Max:* I'm totally crazy. I was
excessed. In Providence. *Prince Max is totally depressed.*
From now on, I will stay here. In the 53rd State of

the Union. I will live in the marshlands. I will cherish the green and pink city in the distance. I will see the cosmoplane light itself up each night.

Nature dreams itself to save itself from truancy, delinquency, and pregnancy.

Chemistry, without training or anesthesia, rebels.

Prince Max puts his hands on his ears and dreams Sibyl.

She is riding across the land. On her horse.
Everything passes out of his mind.

Yet immediately passes back in. There is not going to be
change, Max. There will be even less sympathy. Have you
considered this, Max?

Instead of doing it all, he does none of it.

Hair grows in bad places. Quivery reeds cease to quiver.
Delicate stories cease to matter. There was no narrative.
They left. Bang bang bang like the ten little indians.

"Drop dead."

"I can't."

The abovementioned circumstances taken into consideration, one should suppose that Prince Max would undergo a radical reorientation. He was afraid of thunder and dogs. The dogs were afraid of lightning and the lightning only wanted to be loved. "Knowing is touching," it said as it struck the tree.

Max gets a pet raven. He gives up painting. He writes novels. He eats them for breakfast. Only an eyeball lurks in his eye. His perception is foggy. He lacks authority. He is not punk rock. The raven deserts him. He never had a dog. He is so ugly. He has no pigment to paint with.

He has no indians to dance with. He lost the cabinet. He lost the election, the bones and the feathers. This is the moment that is furthest from awakening.

In his despair he joins the menacing queue. And waits.

boredom boredom boredom boredom
lined interior of boredom
boredom boredom boredom boredom
lined interior of boredom
boredom boredom boredom boredom
lined interior of boredom
boredom boredom boredom boredom
lined interior of boredom

This is the queue.

It's glorified.
It's pacified.
It's one by one the same meted advance: left then right, left then right. In equal measure. Steady, unfaltering.

Max faints in horror and falls from the line.

High above the queue, goslings quiver in the afterlife.
Quiver endlessly in the afterlife of things. Green grow
the rushes. Rushes blow. Marshes stretch from city limit
to state line. If you have ever stepped in a bog you will
understand—the terror. Rushes blow. Goslings quiver.
And stare out at the cosmoverse awaiting . . . anything.

Prince Max dreams nature to escape from himself.
Nature betrays Prince Max and shoots him in the arse
with a finely sharpened reed.

My point is, you're never ready.

Part 2

Time passes quickly too.

Thank the other dimensions for having left you in misery.

Oh every possibility is alive and impregnated.

Deers bell and harbour.

In the capital city,
CAPITALISMUSVILLE,
phantasms slow dance.

I have a dream. Of the 53rd State of the Union. The
buildings are green and the lights are pink. In the
outskirts of the city, hunters prowl, and shoot things.

You feel the burden of tradition lifted.
This is the ice age.
It is tremendously hot.
This is the age of molten lava.

This is the age of magma piles.
This is the age of shingles.
The young are afflicted and the old laugh their asses off.
Then the music stops.

Only snails could love a city.
Only goslings could quiver in the rush.
Only pollen floats.
Only the tree snows.
Only the mountain is buried.
Only the hunters menace the outskirts.
Only the distant field is missing.
My only dream is to be a retired librarian.
My only dream is to have finished everything.
It couldn't be that bad.
It couldn't be a black hole.
It couldn't be a big bad boar.
It couldn't be in Norway, Florida, or New York City.

Hello to you, my friends in Norway:
you know who you are.

Such sad stories are wrapped up in brown paper and syllables.

sing ordac av esc toc pro. shible changee
posset. off wuldd. ized categorke! timlie
words. o be o. t I. for. am rullegabo
derungo endsut of akenvist paro I vent
conated ers willions . comseemy headsof
elf. ion Libal. reiaiam t can a o e o a
wuld ikelisn truct, er, wit. I ions within
I. of. I barm eth disdan wam I . thaplit
I. ay say: nations thank you for you dance

Citywall. Windowseen.
Windowzoom one. Nursemaid and nursed.
"I have to go back to my house."

A terrible sense of unfamiliarity.
As if the universe bifurcated and she was accidentally slid
off "into the wrong one."

Longtime is unforgiving.
She packs a suitcase to go home with.
To that other house from before the forking road.
Windowshades pulled in unfamiliar homes.
In windows throughout the city.

Here's not here.
Track backwards to go home.
Tracking back to known.

step slower
houses go in rows
fires in drums
skywards in backwards
all in a boil
in the wrong kitchen

in recession and regression
in greyhouses folded up in greenhouses

here's not here
's not here
here's not here
not here
's not here

We have to save the prisoners of the old dimentium.
They will lead us home.

The elders of the 53rd State dig up the buried china, the
doll heads, and the room keys.

Cunning o, the rushes grow.

Our dreems
of our dreems
play themselves out
down a one-way street.

But happy things
sing welcome back.

heaadsof elf ions. sing ordac happy
heaadsof elf ions. sing ordac
heaadsof elf ions. sing ordac happy
heaadsof elf ions. sing ordac

Heads in pods. Endless hours.

I am a secret summertime hunter. I am a cunning
collector. An enraptor of things.
A day a day. I'd imagine ether planets other.
A faroffity I'd imagine, or
psychostance. Or distology.

Rabbitology.
Duckitty dog.
Totemic molification.

White over the orange box and nothing but dogstink all
around.

Return to old haunts.
A feast I'll face again.

oh sweet soy
oh duck sauce
oh bird flu

Sing bang! The duck is down.

Diminution of duck faculties.
A duck sauce of ducksong.
Death done.
Duck and gone.

Oh sing praise for things we already understand
and thank god for them
and never leave us, don't, please!

Sing ducksong
to duckgod of thunderquacks.
Then the mirror will discourse on itself:

[COSMOPLANE WALL]

will dance cooomseeemys heaadsof elf ions.
sing ordac av esc toc pro. shchibleee an
po sset. off wuldd. ized categorke! timlie
wor d. be. t i. forg. rull gabo deru mngo e
n dsut fakenvisto paro aeo reiaamo ve iint
conated ers.. ized ion Libal ions. t c aan
wuld ike lisn   truc, ert, wit. I within
I. of. I barm the disdan wam I . thaplit I.
ay say: nat thank ions for you you

[END COSMOPLANE]

It was the beginning and also the end. It was shamefaced and wrong.

A mighty conflict comes. DIS versus DRUID. There is to be no ending. No finality or assignation. No confirmation or condemnation.

But image drifts of druidic duality.
Only here and there.
And always will there be
here and there
but you will be endlessly here.

To know, but never to travel to.
To imagine, but never to reach.

Send signals to other dimmations.

Goslings quiver. They stare across the cosmoplane.
Goslings quiver. They stare across the cosmoplane.

The lightyear calculators drink plum wine and ridicule living things one by one.

Enter Sibyl Kempson from another dimension. She is exhausted from all this entering. She longs for Latin abstractitude. But never tires. In duty. She rides across the land on her horse. She hears things. She shoots moons, which are many. Too much bifurcating. Too much pluraliversing. Snow accumulates on quiet places. No one walks alone tonight. No dog barks alone tonight. No changeling has an inkling. No futures clasp hands. There are warm places to be gotten to. People are having visions of the 58th State. They are jumping ahead. There are mysterious holes in the order of things.

We are in the desert. As you can see.

don't forget the rabbits

"I don't mean to cast stones and all but"

don't forget the rabbits

"abruptly the ground gave way and"

don't forget the rabbits

"everyone above fell below into"

don't forget the rabbits

"THE WARREN"

don't forget the rabbits

"penetrated the deep dark labyrinth"

don't forget the rabbits

"rabbitspliternity, trails and hollows"

don't forget the rabbits

"bifurcating and endless down"

don't forget the rabbits

"they tore everybody's heads off"

foil, foil, foil and trouble
headlessness and headlessness

The door is wide open. Creation was never so constant as this. Nor had it ever worn such a beautiful pink coat.

Some place back in memory, a snail points to a dog who is pointing at the sky in which a bird is headed towards a deer that is pointing at a hunter that is pointing at a rabbit. The rabbit rises up and screams a death curdling gut wringling howl as such did never once come from a rabbit (since the day the prehistoric dinos stepped on all of them). A curdling scream.

So it was that the mighty horde was called into existence. And the hunter became headless
and everything explained.

Still, skeptics sneer at
simple solutions
and unwrap everything that had been neatly wrapped.

A new calendar. Marks a day of holy unwrapping.
Celebrate in Chrysanthemum Square. Six ritual times.

1, 2, 3, 4, 5, 6

Part 3

streaming and differentiation //
bicycle and mandolin //
blueshit and texas //
garbage sack and straddling //
country rock and birding //
lamppost and bookkeeper //
48th and 22nd //
fear and tin foil apothecary //
and cigarette //
clover and after

play zither xylophone yentl veracity
wolvering ethical breakdown
(silence at last)

wolvering ethical breakdown
(triumph at last)

play arthur boring caroline down eerie
freezers (green horned interiors)
silence at last
silence at last

in one of many worlds

gnarled //
humperdinck insidious //
jesuits karlov leskov manifold //
nuisance //
like fifty three //
like none at all //
noisome operating pullmanist

parceling quivering //
rascally snoop //
like acts of rescue equal a flood //
equals ten thousand bales of hay

tivoli ursus voidal wolvering ethical breakdown

Silence at last.
Silence at last.

c o o o mseeemys a h e o a dsf elf. sing
ions. o rad c av an esc at toc at pro.
shchibleee. po e t. wu l. s s d d. izieid
c e aan ke! tmlie wor d. be. t. fg. bg a o
or deru mngo e n dsut fak e n a p rrrr vis
t o o f f eiaam ooeaove iint conated ers.
ized Liion balions. rullwul k d tru sln c,
ert, go wit. I. of. I bam the disdan wam I
. h a t c plit t Ii e. a ys n a ys thank ion
youi for you within I I will dance.

Armies are moving. The rabbit horde is in for an ass-kicking.

The men of the North and the men of the South will round up the rabbits with bayonets. They will back them up against a cliff. And the rabbits will drop. They will hop to their long, to the way, across the wintry and tundrally wasteland, falling downside cliffside and taken up by cosmic winds. Blown all the way to Rabbit's Hole, where dead things are passed out of the cosmoverse and passed in to the uniplane, which is before and after all things.

Sibyl, Sibyl, whisperings Gosling Mary. *I have lost my rabbit love. You must away to Rabbit's Hole to rescue his soul before he migrates into the undimmation.*

And how will I find the rabbit's soul?
by traveling quick to rabbit hole
And how will I know the Rabbit Hole?
you must ask the vole

The vole, who lives in a tunnel by the observatory, takes Sibyl to the telescope. He does not know where to find

Rabbit's Hole, but he knows how to look for it. During the night, Sibyl swivels the scope about and looks at other worlds. Sibyl, what do you see?

Sibyl swings the scope and speaks:

I see a world in which the revolutionary rabbit has been
enthroned. He sits in a pale damp room of the palace. His
drooping eyes roll images of the land back and forth in
a half sleep; he has become everything he fought against.
The palace bears down on the vegetation. The headless,
who have undergone voluntary rehabilitation, are planted
in orderly rows in the palace gardens. Metabolic energy
lies in submission. This world is calm: limestone calm.
But the rabbit is old. Murmurs between the blossoms of
the headless trees.

Sibyl swings the scope and speaks:

Now I see another rabbit world, where Augustus B. Rabbit walks down graceful colonnades hand in hand with a lightyear calculator. Their pace is slow. They're talking about the stars, about the birth of the stars and the end of the universe. The rows of headless trees have blossomed. The goslings perch in the lower branches and dive into duckponds.

Sibyl swings the scope and speaks:

Another rabbit world. The rebellion has succeeded. A repellant dome was constructed to keep the lightyear calculators at bay. The young meet in the corners, they're tired of enforced cooperation. Rumors circulate of a passionate love affair between a young rabbit and a lightyear calculator. The old revolutionary council of rabbits struggle to maintain the purity of their defiance. Headquartered on a neighboring star, the lightyear calculators scan the dome daily, looking for the crack that will inevitably appear.

Sibyl swings the scope and speaks:

Another rabbit world. Augustus B. commands the
rebel rabbits from deep in the woods around the city.
The palace is heavily fortified. There are constant
explosions. Bombs explode in green sewers. Hovering
bands of rabbits descend without warning, met by
terrible bands of unclear association. The lightyear
calculators have all convened in the palace; they stare
nervously out the windows and grimace. The gangs
they have sent to combat the rabbits have morphed into
something perverse and unaffiliated. It is a steady state
of emergency, rebellion and response. And the polleny
ponds, goslings quiver, fearful of everything.

Still, rabbits are less fearsome than sturgeon, triceratops,
unicorns, voles, wildebeest, xifa, yellowtails, zaurinebras.
But what is more fearsome than a neverending
deathwaltz?

boredom boredom boredom

Save us Sibyl.
Kill the lightyear calculators.
Make it all stop traveling.
Make it rest.

Part 4
Epitaph

COSMOPLANE WALL, gently:

the ends of times discourse on themselves.

sing ions. o ra d c av an esc a t t t t. th oc at
pro.
shchili b l e e e. po o o o o o o o et.

cavan esacpt, headself. pote.

wulll will macks l. s d d. izieid c e n ke!
t m e wor d. be. fg. bg a o or deru m m n go e n
dsu

fak e n a p rrrr v i s t f f

vista, elf cont en ders, pote: I the disdan wam.
ei a a a an ion y ui wit I. I d   an e.

a zed. an ion. a pote. a poet headelf the disdan
wam. will to you, to my word. to my foggy, bog
words. vist, fake words. conated willions. a
zed, the end, beheaded pote. for some things must

die so that others can. caravand. foggy, boggy.
fake words, con willions. fake vistas, go wit. er.
will dance, the disdan wam. some things die so
that others can wam. the disdan beginning of the
middle of the end, the dane, the dan, the beheaded
bend. so all can wam. fake endings, fake vistas:
the cosmoplane the caravan the disdan wam.

mighty ions go sliptaparting over the whole of
space and nothing is ending. it flies off, it binds
back, to the origin of the smallest divergence.
The earliest future of measurement. Because a
curve is a line in motion that is bound to its
point of origin. A curve is a line in motion that
loves its rabbit mom.

DEATH TO THE LIGHTYEAR CALCULATORS!

release the ion bonds

and elf contenders sing to max, and max sings to
goslings, and goslings sing of a green and pink
city and a curving surface of-

starts

just look at them   just look at them

stars   just look at them

                    look at them

          starts

just look at them just look at them

stars   just look at them

          just look at them

starts

                              just look at them

                just look at them

stars
just look at them

        look at them

stars

just look at them

look at them

ASTRS was written in the spring of 2005. Source materials, locations, and patron saints include Walter Benjamin's *Arcades Project*, with emphasis on the passages on Louis Auguste Blanqui; Michael Taussig; a beloved falafel spot called The Lite Touch on A; Ulla Dydo's account in *The Language That Rises* of Gertrude Stein's process of writing by looking at her local radius day after day until a notebook was full; fellow lemurians Sibyl Kempson and Laura Jones; and presiding wooden-headed genie of the Barker Room, Mac Wellman, who might have likened this text to a painting with a fairy splitting another one's head with an axe. Or did he say that about a totally different play?

ASTRS WAS PERFORMED:

In Little Theater at Tonic, with Kristen Kosmas, Heidi
Schreck, David Neumann and Steven Rattazzi;

At Dixon Place on the Bowery, performed by David
Neumann, Heidi Schreck, Katy Pyle and Karinne Keithley
with video dances and photography performances by
Sibyl Kempson and Andrew Dinwiddie, video recitations
by Steven Rattazzi and Normandy Sherwood, drawings
and costumes by Sara Smith, and stop motion animations
by KK made in a toy theater full of hunters and deer and
green and pink cities made by Gina Siepel;

As a live-drawn mural by the posse Joyce Cho at the
Prelude Festival 2008, supported by a residency at Five
Myles, with drawings by the Chos (Scott Adkins, Kelly
Copper, Rob Erickson, KK, Sibyl Kempson, Amber Reed)
plus Erin Courtney and Ethan Hanson, bunny cookies by
Amber Reed, and all embedded into—

—a radio play recorded by KK and voiced by Scott Ad-
kins, Kate Benson, Erin Courtney, Rob Erickson, Karinne
Keithley, Sibyl Kempson, Amber Reed, Jenny Seastone
Stern, and Sara Walsh, with underscoring and music by
KK and Lumberob—

—and said radio play was broadcast on The Acousmatic Theater Hour on WFMU, November 2, 2008.

IT'S TRUE THAT ASTRS is the origin of the 53rd State and namesake of this press, and also that this text is published to mark the occasion of founding editor Karinne Keithley Syers' abandonment of her post, having gratefully relayed her duties to a new KK. Over & out.

53rd STATE PRESS

A New Practical Guide to Rhetorical Gesture and Action // NTUSA
A Field Guide to iLANDing // iLAND
The 53rd State Occasional No. 2 // Ed. Will Arbery
Suicide Forest // Haruna Lee
Rude Mechs' Lipstick Traces // Lana Lesley + the Rude Mechs
MILTON // PearlDamour
The People's Republic of Valerie, Living Room Edition // Kristen Kosmas
uncollected trash collection // Kate Kremer
A Discourse on Method // David Levine + Shonni Enelow
Severed // Ignacio Lopez
Ann, Fran, and Mary Ann // Erin Courtney
Love Like Light // Daniel Alexander Jones
Particle and Wave: A Conversation // Daniel Alexander Jones + Alexis Pauline Gumbs
ASTRS // Karinne Keithley Syers
The Lost Conversation // Sara Farrington

FORTHCOMING

SKiNFoLK: An American Show // Jillian Walker
Angela's Mixtape/The History of Light // Eisa Davis
Eisa Davis + Jillian Walker: Two Conversations // Davis + Walker
WATER SPORTS; or insignificant white boys // Jeremy O. Harris
I Understand Everything Better // Advanced Beginner Group
Wood Calls Out to Wood // Corinne Donly
Karen Davis // Jess Barbagallo
Broken Clothing // Suzanne Bocanegra

ABOUT THE PRESS

53rd State Press publishes lucid, challenging, and lively new writing for performance. Our catalog includes new plays as well as scores and notations for interdisciplinary performance, graphic adaptations, and essays on theater and dance.

53rd State Press was founded in 2007 by Karinne Keithley in response to the bounty of new writing in the downtown New York community that was not available except in the occasional reading or short-lived performance. In 2010, Antje Oegel joined her as a co-editor. In 2018, Kate Kremer took on the leadership of the volunteer editorial collective. For more information or to order books, please visit 53rdstatepress.org.

53rd State Press books are represented to the trade by TCG (Theatre Communications Group). TCG books are exclusively distributed to the book trade by Consortium Book Sales and Distribution, an Ingram Brand.

LAND & LABOR ACKNOWLEDGMENTS

53rd State Press recognizes that much of the work we publish was first developed and performed on the unceded lands of the Lenape and Canarsie communities. Our books are stored on and shipped from the unceded lands of the Chickasaw, Cherokee, Shawnee, and Yuchi communities. The work that we do draws on natural resources that members of the Indigenous Diaspora have led the way in protecting and caretaking. We are grateful to these Indigenous communities, and commit to supporting Indigenous-led movements working to undo the harms of colonization.

As a press devoted to preserving the ephemeral experiments of the contemporary avant-garde, we recognize with great reverence the work of radical BIPOC artists whose (often uncompensated) experiments have been subject to erasure, appropriation, marginalization, and theft. We commit to amplifying the revolutionary experiments of earlier generations of BIPOC theatermakers, and to publishing, promoting, celebrating, and compensating the BIPOC playwrights and performers revolutionizing the field today.

ASTRS is made possible by the New York State Council on the Arts with the support of Governor Andrew M. Cuomo and the New York State Legislature.

NEW YORK
STATE OF
OPPORTUNITY.

Council on
the Arts

53rd State Press
new writing for performance